Shahrukh Salman

Effects of Perceived Service Quality on Customer Loyalty and Repurchase Intentions

The Mediating Role of Customer Satisfaction

Anchor Academic
Publishing

Salman, Shahrukh: Effects of Perceived Service Quality on Customer Loyalty and Repurchase Intentions. The Mediating Role of Customer Satisfaction, Hamburg, Anchor Academic Publishing 2017

Buch-ISBN: 978-3-96067-187-9
PDF-eBook-ISBN: 978-3-96067-687-4
Druck/Herstellung: Anchor Academic Publishing, Hamburg, 2017

Bibliografische Information der Deutschen Nationalbibliothek:
Die Deutsche Nationalbibliothek verzeichnet diese Publikation in der Deutschen Nationalbibliografie; detaillierte bibliografische Daten sind im Internet über http://dnb.d-nb.de abrufbar.

Bibliographical Information of the German National Library:
The German National Library lists this publication in the German National Bibliography. Detailed bibliographic data can be found at: http://dnb.d-nb.de

© Anchor Academic Publishing, Imprint der Diplomica Verlag GmbH
Hermannstal 119k, 22119 Hamburg
http://www.diplomica-verlag.de, Hamburg 2017
Printed in Germany

ACKNOWLEDGEMENT

We are extremely thankful to ALLAH Al-Mighty, the most beneficial and merciful, who gave us knowledge, power and courage to complete this project. We are also thankful to our advisor Mr. Ahmed-Ur-Rehman for helping us extensively through-out the project whenever we needed. Without his help and guidance, it could not be possible for us to complete this project.

We would also like to acknowledge our parents, brothers and sisters for their cooperation and useful help during the research project.

Although feelings are deep but unfortunately the words are too shallow. That cannot follow the depth of our feelings. We feel no way to convey our gratitude to our benefactors so we have gone through the old conventional way. The name has been mentioned but the extent and sibilance of their help is impossible to capture.

Abstract

The primary objective of this study is to gage the affect of perceived service quality on customer loyalty and repurchase intentions through customer satisfaction. In this study it is explained the significance of customer satisfaction on customer loyalty and repurchase intentions. Customer satisfactions play the mediating role between perceived service qualities, customer loyalty and repurchase intentions. Population of the research is potential customers of Lahore and the sample size is 230. Results has been drawn by using regression analysis which showed significant relationships between perceived service quality and customer satisfaction, customer satisfaction and customer loyalty, customer satisfaction and repurchase intentions, perceived service quality and repurchase intentions. This study suggests that emphasis should be given on service quality as it is a key variable that enhances customer satisfaction and leads to customer loyalty and repurchase intentions. This in return generates profitability for the food/restaurant industry.

Keywords: Perceived Service quality, Customer satisfaction, and Customer Loyalty and Repurchase Intentions.

Table of Contents

LIST OF TABLES

LIST OF FIGURES

LIST OF APPENDICES

1. INTRODUCTION

Introduction

In today's era of competitive environment, service quality is the major focus of the service providers. Past researchers have showed that evaluations of service quality have close positive relation with customer loyalty and behavioral intentions (Zeithaml, Berry & Parasuraman, 1996). In food industry, service managers have a great focus on generating customer satisfaction and customer loyalty. The focus of this research study is to examine how much is the impact of the customer satisfaction in order to generate customer loyalty and repurchase intentions by continuously improving service quality.

The research intends to study the relationship of four concepts i.e. perceived service quality, Customer Satisfaction, Loyalty and Repurchase Intentions. According to researchers, the index of the success of an organization resulting in productive benefits is the advantage of satisfaction and quality benefit (Ruyter, 1997). Yet another research admits that service loyalty which eventually wins customers and results in repeated purchases by loyal buyers is the base of service marketing; realistically, those consumers who make regular purchases form the basis of any business (Caruana, 2002).

Service industries are playing a pivotal role in developing the economies of all the countries across the world, services are contributing more than 60% in the economies of the developing countries (Lien-Ti Bei, 2001). The study of service quality and customer satisfaction have been the dominant variables in the service literature gathered so far (Cronin, Brandy & Hult, 2000). Parasuraman, Zeithaml and Barry (1985) gave the well accepted five-gap service model (intangibility, responsiveness, reliability, assurance, empathy) that became the forefront and the guiding principal for the services related research (Lien-Ti Bei, 2001).

Past research has proved that service quality is an antecedent of customer satisfaction which leads to customer loyalty (Cronin et al., 2000; Oliver, 1999; Zeithaml, 1988). The objective of our study is to find the effect of perceived service quality and customer satisfaction on customer loyalty and repurchase intentions. However the study conducted will give some more insight into the existing study.

Objectives / Purpose of the project

The objective of this research is to learn the relationship between customer's perception about the services of the organization which will have an effect on its satisfaction level and generates loyalty and lead to repurchase intension.

This research will explain the theoretical frameworks which are developed i.e. perceived service quality as an independent variable; loyalty and repurchase intentions as dependant variables. Customer satisfaction mediates between independent (Perceived Service Quality) and dependent variables (Loyalty & Repurchase Intentions). With the help of this study; the perception of customers about service quality in restaurants will be found. The satisfaction level will have a significant relationship with loyalty of the customers and their repurchase intentions.

Basically the study altogether is about the behavior of the customers to find whether the customers are satisfied with the services of the organization and are they up to their standards.

2. LITERATURE REVIEW

Literature Review

Perceived service quality

Service quality was defined in past as the disparity between the expectation and perception of service which is received or to be received by the customers (Gronroos, 2001). Parasuraman et al., (1985) has explained that perceived service quality is the comparison of what services are being offered by the service provider and what they actually should be.

Service was defined by Gronroos (2000) as, "A service is a process consisting of a series of more or less intangible activities that normally, but not necessarily always, take place in interactions between the customer and service employees and/or physical resources or goods and/or systems of the service provider, which are provided as solutions to the customer problems". Service Quality was however defined by Fogli (2006) as "A global judgement or attitude relating to a particular service; the customer's overall impression of the relative inferiority or superiority of the organization and its services. Service quality is a cognitive judgement". Service quality has become so important that this is considered an important strategy to be implemented for success in present competitive environment (Parasuraman et al., 1985; Reichheld and Sasser, 1990; Zeithmal et al., 1996). In a study, Buzzell and Gale (1987) have discussed that those companies who focus on delivering better service quality achieve greater market share and high growth. With superior service quality delivery the profits increased because of greater market share and growth. (Bagozzi & Philips, 1982)

Parasuraman et al., (1985) has defined perceived service quality as "a global judgment, or attitude" relating to superiority of a service". Asubonteng, McCleary and Swan (1996), has defined service Quality as "the difference between customer expectations for service performance prior to the service encounter and their perception of the service perceived".

There are a few features of the services which were identified by Mudie and Pirrie (2006) which are discussed below:

Intangibility: It is one of the main features of service. Service does not have a tangible identity that means that it cannot be touched, counted, tested, verified or measured as in the case of sale of goods. This is one of the main reasons that most of the companies and organizations find it very hard to evaluate their services or the quality of their services.

Inseparability (simultaneous production and consumption): This is again a quality that hugely differentiates the physical goods from services. Services are produced, sold and consumed at the same time whereas the tangible products or goods are first produced than sold and consumed at the end.

Variability (heterogeneity): Variability and heterogeneity is also one of the important features of services. As services are provided by different people and all have different temperament and way of thinking therefore the services they provide are also unique in their respect. The quality however may vary depending upon the person who is providing these services and it also very much depends upon how these services are provided.

Perishability: Services are also perishable in nature as they cannot be stored because they are performances. We cannot store the services with an intention of using them at a later stage as they are consumed at the time they are produced.

In today's competitive competition that is going on in the business world service quality is considered as the major tool that helps the organizations gain competitive advantage over other organizations. This also is the major differentiator that differentiates the two service organizations. Some past references of the different studies say that service quality fulfills the need and expectations of the customers (Dotchin & Oakland, 1994). Parasuraman et al., (1985) highlighted that "the judgment on service quality is a reflection of the degree and direction of discrepancy between consumer's perception and expectations." By providing good service quality; organizations can achieve customer satisfaction, customer loyalty, and repurchase intentions (Hackl, Scharitzer & Zuba, 2000).

In service marketing literature, the conceptualization and measurement of perceived service quality is the most argued and debatable topic (Zeithmal, 2000; Rust & Oliver, 2000).

Services are intangible and the consumer's asses the services subjectively which is why service quality is referred as obscure and indefinable. (Parasuraman et al., 1985; Smith, 1999).

In literature, many varieties of quality models are available. SERVQUAL MODEL is one of the most widely used models which are developed by Parasuraman, Zeithamal & Berry, (1988). Reliability, responsiveness, empathy, assurance, and tangibility are the five dimensions postulated in SERVQUAL Model. Reliability means an ability of any organization in providing promised services accurately and correctly. Assurance looks up to the knowledge of employees and their capability to pass on reliance and confidence. Tangibles refer to the physical entities of any organization. Empathy means providing individual attention and responsiveness is the willingness of employees in providing help and prompt services to their customers.

Customer loyalty

Loyalty is defined by Gremler and Brown (1996) as "the degree to which a customer exhibits purchasing behavior from a service Provider, processes a positive attitudinal disposition toward the provider, and considers using only this provider when a need for this service arises".

Loyalty is the willingness of the customer to utilize the same services provider/service company consistently, that maybe preferred among other alternatives, thus in compliance of actual behavioral outcome and favorable attitudes, regardless of marketing efforts and situational influences which are made to stimulate switching behavior(Caruana, 1999; Gremler & Brown, 1996). Zeithaml (1996) argues the dimensions of loyalty in his study, such as willingness to pay more and loyalty under increased pricing which have mostly been left out in past researches. Furthermore, loyalty has often been devised in positive terms; however, variables which predict the positive outcomes may be related to those variables that predict the disloyalty of the customers (Zeithaml, 1996). Perceived service quality is often viewed as a key antecedent of service loyalty (Dick & Basu, 1994). Oliver (1999) has conceptualized that firstly customer should be at the stage of "cognitive loyalty", in which customer become loyal because of belief in brand and prior knowledge. Second stage is affective loyalty in which customer becomes loyal because of frequent usage or interaction. Third is the conative stage in which customers does not persuade from alternatives and have hold strong loyal repurchase intentions.

Loyalty as defined by many researchers is that it is based on two concepts one is customer attitude and other is behaviors; customer attitudes contain repurchase intention or purchasing same products and service again from the same company and refer the company to other customers (Narayandas, 1996). There is a strong relationship between Service quality and customer loyalty knowing that these have different meanings and values according to the customer (Sureshchanndra, Rajendran & Anantharaman, 2002). As defined by Johnson and hart (1999), if a customer is loyal to any company he is completely satisfied as well. Most of the studies conducted give us more than two ways to generate customer loyalty that are to delight customers and to provide excellent service and best Products (Lee & Feick, 2001). From Attitudinal point of view customer loyalty is desire to start make and continue a relation with any service provider (Czepiel & Gilmore, 1987). Customer loyalty as per behavioral point of view is that if a buyer buys a same product or service every time it shows that the customer is loyal to that particular product or service (Neal, 1999). Loyalty can be beneficial for both customer and the Company if the customers make themselves completely loyal to one particular company. This can benefit customer that he is valued client of that company and company will offer its customer the best possible rates in the competitive market (Reichheld, 1996).

Customer satisfaction

Customer perception of the received value results in the satisfaction of the customer (Hallowell, 1996). Perceived service quality is the first major factor of customer satisfaction where as the second factor is perceived value of the product (Fornell, 1996). Customer satisfaction is truly based on the price paid and value received against the price (Athanassopoulos, 2000). Service quality perception leads to the customer satisfaction which shows a psitive relation (Bagozzi, 1992). Service quality and customer satisfaction are directly attached with the customer loyalty and repurchase intentions leads to customer loyalty as well (Levesque & MC Dougall, 1996). Customer loyalty can be achieved through excellent service quality which is the goal of the organization (Ehigie, 2006). Good service quality gives the customer satisfaction, and customer loyalty can be achieved through customer satisfaction (Carvana 2002) Customer satisfaction and customer loyalty have direct relationship between

9

them (Ehigie 2006). Customer satisfaction defined by transaction specific approach as the recent experience in dealing with a company shows a good response or an unfavorable response (Oliver, 1993). Some of the researchers define that overall satisfaction of a customer is depending upon Perceived service quality. If we view the behavior of the customer (Repurchase intention), the overall satisfaction lies on what a customer thinks about a company, if it is in good response it will lead to a better customer loyalty (Cronin & Tylor, 1992).

Perceived service quality and customer satisfaction are different constructs (Oliver, 1997; Taylor & Baker, 1994). There is a causal relationship between perceived service quality and customer satisfaction (Cronin & Taylor, 1992; Gotlieb, Grewal & Brown, 1994; Spreng & Mackoy, 1996). Perceived service quality may be defined as the customer long term cognitive evaluations of a company's service delivery whereas customer satisfaction is a short term emotional response to performance of a specific service (Lovelock & Wright, 1999). In some cases, these constructs have been used interchangeably (Iacobuc, Grayson & Ostrom, 1994; Taylor & Baker, 1994; Oliver, 1997; Mittal, Ross & Baldasare, 1998).

Generally, perceived service quality and customer satisfaction are assessment or review variables which are related to customer judgments about the product (Iacobuci et al., 1994; Oliver, 1997).

Zeithmal and Bitner, (2003) have defined satisfaction as the "fulfillment" response of the consumers. It is believed that either the product or service or any feature of the product or service provides the congenial level of fulfillment after consumption. SERVQUAL model proposes satisfaction a broader concept of service quality.

H1:   Perceived service quality has a relationship with customer satisfaction

Loyalty is the outcome variable in service quality models (Cronin & Taylor, 1992), but there are many aspects that limit thorough understanding of customer loyalty in services and confine the general ability of research outcomes.

Cronin and Taylor (1992), focused only on repurchase intentions (assuming this construct as a single item), whereas Boulding, Staelin & Zeithaml (1993) focused on repurchase intentions and willingness to recommend (as two single items in one study). This study examines the direct impact of perceived service quality on customer loyalty.

H2:   Perceived service quality has a relationship with customer Loyalty

Customer satisfaction management has emerged strategically important for most firms in the past two decades (Honomichl, 1993). Firms switched their goals towards achieving higher satisfactory ratings in 1980's (Wall Street Journal 1998). It was realized only in 1990's that customer satisfaction ratings indicated customer retention which directly affected the profits of a firm or company (Jones & Sasser 1995; Reichheld, 1996). Due to this fact a lot of firms allocated a lot of resources to understand how satisfaction was directly affecting customer retention (Bolton, 1998). This focus is necessary because it is a universally accepted rule that cost of retaining a customer is much less than cost of attracting a new customer, not only this the new customer costs a company much more than the older customers (Richheld, 1996). To examine the relationship between customer satisfactions and repurchase intentions we have postulated a hypothesis; stated below.

H3:   Customer satisfaction has a relationship with repurchase intentions

The most commonly defined definition by most of the authors is that a satisfaction is a feeling of a customer what really is he expecting and what he is getting along with the loyalty which us shown through purchase intensions and fulfillment of needs and wants as well (Armstrong & Kotler,1996). The literature gathered from service management shows us that customer satisfaction results from the perception of customer against the value received in a particular transaction or a relationship- here value is equal to the perceived service quality and costs of customer acquisition (Blanchard & Galloway, 1994)- compared to value expected from the competing brands or similar companies (Zeithaml et al., 1990). All the different kinds of behavior that show loyalty including continuance relationship, increased sales or scope of relationship, and recommendations are a result of customers feeling and belief that a particular vendor is providing more value with regards to money compared to other similar vendors. Loyalty which is formed in all different styles mentioned above gives a firm a lot of profits because the cost of attracting the new customers is a lot more than retaining the existing customers also a firm has to spend a lot less on existing customers as compared to the new customers (Reicheld & Sasser, 1990).

Yi's "Critical Review of Customer Satisfaction" (1990) concludes, "Many studies found that customer satisfaction influences purchase intentions as well as post-purchase attitude".

The customer Loyalty can be defined in two different ways according to the marketing literature (Jacoby & Kyner, 1973). The first way says that loyalty is attitude of a customer. The feelings of a customer are mainly responsible for a customer's attachment to a particular organization, product or service (Fornier, 1994).

The second way loyalty has been defined is in terms of the customer behavior. This means the general tendency of a person to buy a particular product from the same supplier; this in turn is responsible for increasing the relationship bondage. This is the same view as the concept has been described in the service management literature.

To examine the relationship between customer satisfaction and customer loyalty we have formulated following hypothesis:

H4:   Customer satisfaction has a relationship with Customer loyalty

Loyalty for service field cannot be generalized with previous findings of tangible products' loyalty. It is yet to be explored in service field as there is a huge opportunity for research with two obvious loopholes. Firstly, most of the research work has done on how perceived service quality affect service loyalty. In order to find out effect of service loyalty on customer satisfaction, more focused researches are required to be done to assess service loyalty (Clark & Wood, 1998).

Secondly the construct of service loyalty has ambiguous operationalization and most of them focus on the behavioral (Dawes & Swailes , 1999; DeSouza, 1992; Disney, 1999; Guolla & Large, 1997; Hallowell, 1996; Kendrick,1998; Loveman, 1998; Zeithaml et al.,1996) and attitudinal measure (Bloemer & Kasper., 1995; Czepiel and Gilmore, 1987). Service Loyalty varies from industry to industry, different measures are taken for different service industries.

Measure of Service Loyalty and conceptualization can be classified into three phases. Initially, customer loyalty was defined by the researchers and marketers as the behavior of customers towards service providers/service companies (Jacoby & Chestnut, 1978). Measurement of loyalty should not only include purchase behavior pattern (Andreassen & Linderstad, 1998), but also the attitude of the customer (O' Malley, 1988). However this statement does not imply that only attitudinal measure should be included to gage customer loyalty (O' Malley, 1988). This will simplify that the unsatisfied customer will switch its preferences for other alternatives and satisfied customer will be loyal (O' Malley, 1988).

In second phase, researchers measured customer loyalty by integrating attitudinal and behavioral measures simultaneously. Sustainable loyalty can be accomplished with high level of re-utilizing pattern and high level of positive attitude (Dick & Basu, 1994)

In third phase, measure of service loyalty has been classified into three traits; i.e. Behavioral, attitudinal and cognitive. In order to Create and develop long term service loyalty service providers/companies need to ensure customer satisfaction as perceived quality is insufficient to build long term loyalty without mediating effect of customer satisfaction.

Research has emphasized that service Loyalty is classified into three aspect; Behavioral, attitudinal and cognitive. To engage loyal customers, organizations need to devise separate strategies for three different kinds of customers interacting with them.

Repurchase intentions repeatedly show the continuous commitment (Shemwell, Yavas & Bilgin, 1998) and loyal attitude of the customers towards service providers/ service companies (Cunningham, 1956).

H5:   Perceived service quality has a relationship with repurchase intentions

H6:   Customer satisfaction mediates the relationship between perceived service quality and loyalty

H7:   Customer satisfaction mediates the relationship between perceived service quality and repurchase intentions.

Theoretical Framework

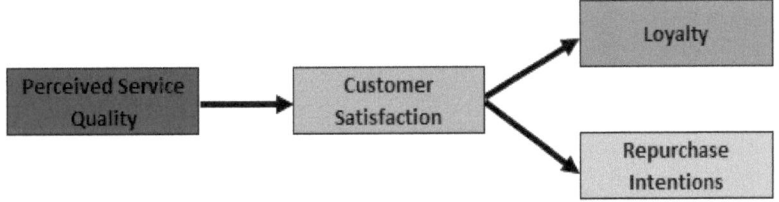

3. RESEARCH METHODOLOGY

Research methodology

The industry selected for this research study is restaurants and the population is customers of Lahore. The data will be collected from 230 respondents. We will use non probability sampling technique, in which we'll go for convenient sampling. Data was gathered by means of convenient sampling with the help of questionnaires in Lahore city of Pakistan. A total of 300 questionnaires were distributed out of which 250 questionnaire were returned back with response rate of 83.3%. We found 230 usable questionnaires, remaining questionnaire were incomplete.

Measures

Following are the measures which are undertaken for this research study:

Perceived service quality: Dimensions were operational on the basis of 22 items with 7 point likert scale by Zeithaml, Parasuraman and Berry (1988). Each of the items is accompanied by a seven-point scale ranging from 1 = strongly disagree to 7 = strongly agree, item like "Restaurant's physical facilities are visually appealing".

Customer satisfaction: 17 Item Scale with 7 point liker scale by Gilbert, Cleopatra & Goodeand, (2006). All items are escorted by a seven-point scale ranging from 1 = strongly disagree to 7 = strongly agree, item like "The service provided by the restaurant is on time".

Customer loyalty: 7 item Scale with 7 point likert scale by Zeithaml, Parasuraman and Berry, (1996). Each item is measured by a seven-point scale ranging from 1 = strongly disagree to 7 = strongly agree, item like "I believe that this is my favorite restaurant".

Repurchase intentions: 2 Item scale with 7 point likert scale by Cronin & Taylor, (1992). Each of the items is measured by a seven-point scale ranging from 1 = strongly disagree to 7 = strongly agree, item like "I intend to continue to be customer of this restaurant".

4. RESULTS

Results

In this study, we have included demographics and restaurant preference as control variables. The sample is representative of the population of Lahore city in Pakistan on the basis of demographic criteria such as age, gender, qualification and income. The responses are gathered from male (60%) and female (40%); majority of the customers fall between 15 to 25 years of age (63.9 %), rest of the customers were between 26-35 years of age (33.5%), 36-45 years of age (1.7%) and 46-55 years of age (0.9). Income of the respondents varied between 15-30K-PKR (44.3%), 30-45K-PKR (20.4%), and 45-60K-PKR (16.1%) and above 60 K-PKR (19.1%). Preferences of restaurants resulted as Nandoos (26.1%), Pizza Hutt (25.2%), Bundu Khan (12.2%), Village (10.4%), Fazal –e-Haq (10%) , HsinKong (5.7%) Dhabba and MeiKong (5.2%).

In regards to perceived service quality, customer satisfaction, customer loyalty and repurchase intentions following means are obtained: Age; 1.39 (S.D .57), Gender; 1.40 (S.D .49), Income; 2.10 (S.D 1.16), Restaurants 5.05 (S.D 2.38).

Table 1
Correlation Analysis

	Mean	S.D	1.Gender	2.Age	3.Qualification	4.Income	5.Restaurant	6.PSQMean	7.CSMean	8.CLMean	9.RIMean
1.Gender	1.40	.49									
2.Age	1.39	.57	-.20**								
3.Qualification	1.90	.71	-.08	.59**							
4.Income	2.10	1.16	-.21**	.30**	.39**						
5.Restarurant	5.05	2.38	.06	-.08	.04	-.07					
6.Perceived Service Quality	5.14	.77	.02	.29**	.38**	.09	.13*	(.92)			
7.Customer Satisfaction	5.16	.76	.04	.21**	.31**	.12	.13*	.81**	(.91)		
8.Loyalty	4.77	.95	.14	.15*	.20**	.16*	.09	.52**	.60**	(.81)	
9.Repurchase Intention	5.21	1.04	.05	.09	.22**	.22**	.15*	.48**	.53**	.67**	(.75)

*. Correlation is significant at the 0.05 level (2-tailed).
**. Correlation is significant at the 0.01 level (2-tailed).
() α Cronbach's Alpha

Table 1

Results shows that correlation between perceived service quality and customer satisfaction scores are r=.81 (p= .00). Correlation between perceived service quality and loyalty scores are r=.52 (p= .00), correlation between Customer Satisfaction and Customer Loyalty scores are r=.60 (p= .00), correlation between Perceived Service Quality and Repurchase Intention scores are r=.58 (p= .00), correlation between Customer Satisfaction and Repurchase Intention scores are r=.53 (p= .00).

TABLE 2								
Regression Analysis								
	Customer satisfaction			Customer Loyalty			Repurchase Intentions		
	B	R2	P	B	R2	P	B	R2	P
Perceived Service Quality	.81	.66	.0 0	.52	.27	.00	.58	.23	.00
Customer Satisfaction				.60	.37	.00	.53	.28	.00

Table 2

Tables 2 summarize the results of the regression analysis of perceived service quality on customer satisfaction, customer loyalty and repurchase intentions. As hypothesized, perceived service quality has a relationship with customer satisfaction where $R^2 = .66$, ($\beta = .81$, p=.00) which shows that Perceived Service Quality has 66% significant impact on Customer Satisfaction. Hence hypothesis 1 is accepted. Perceived Service quality with customer loyalty where $R^2 = .27$, ($\beta = .52$, p=.00) which shows that Perceived Service Quality has 27% significant impact on Customer Loyalty, hence hypothesis 2 is accepted and customer satisfaction with repurchase intentions where $R^2 = .28$, ($\beta = .53$, p=.00) which shows that Customer Satisfaction has 28% significant impact on Repurchase Intention, hence hypothesis 3 is accepted. In consistence with hypothesis 1, 2 & 3, customer satisfaction has a relationship with customer loyalty where $R^2 = .37$, ($\beta = .60$, p=.00) which shows that Customer Satisfaction has 37% significant impact on Customer Loyalty, hence hypothesis 4 is accepted. Relationship between perceived service quality and repurchase intentions has been proven significance where $R^2 = .23$, ($\beta = .58$, p=.00) which shows that Perceived Service Quality has 23% significant impact on Repurchase Intention, hence hypothesis 5 is accepted.

Mediation analysis

According to Baron and Kenny, (1986), three conditions should be followed:

- Independent variable has a significant relationship with Mediating variable
- Mediating variable has a significant relationship with Dependant variable
- Independent variable has a significant relationship with Dependant variable

As these relationships are significant & hypothesis 1,2,3,4, & 5 are accepted according to the three conditions so we will check the mediation i.e,

H1: Perceived service quality has a relationship with customer satisfaction. H2: Perceived service quality has a relationship with customer loyalty. H3: Customer satisfaction has a relationship with Repurchase intention. H4: Customer satisfaction has a relationship with Customer loyalty. H5: Perceived service quality has a relationship with Repurchase intention.

	Customer Loyalty				Repurchase Intentions			
	β	R2	ΔR2	P	B	R2	ΔR2	P
Perceived Service Quality	.52	.27		.00	.58	.23		.00
STEP1 **Customer Satisfaction**	.60	.37		.00	.53	.28		.00
STEP 2 **Perceived Service Quality**	.08	.37	.003	.33	.01	.29	.007	.14

Table 3 — Mediation Analysis

Table 3

According to Baron and Kenny, (1986) two conditions should be followed to prove the mediation:

- Change in R^2 must approach to 0
- β should be insignificant

Hypothesis 6, which reveals that customer satisfaction, mediates the relationship between perceived service quality and customer loyalty where $\Delta R^2 = .003$ i.e., .3% (β = .08, p=.33, $\Delta R^2 = .003$). Hence both the conditions are met and it is full mediation so hypothesis 6 is accepted.

Hypothesis 7, which reveals that customer satisfaction, mediates the relationship between perceived service quality and repurchase intention where $\Delta R^2 = .007$ i.e., .7% (β = .01, p=.14, $\Delta R^2 = .007$). Hence both the conditions are met and it is full mediation so hypothesis 7 is accepted.

5. DISCUSSION & CONCLUSION

Discussion & conclusion

The findings of this research study reveal that the significance of relationship between perceived service quality and customer satisfaction is consistent with the expectations and previous research as supported by earlier research conducted by Namkung & Jang, (2007).

This research has examined the relationship of perceived service quality and customer Satisfaction and the repurchase intentions in the restaurants. The findings of this research support the hypothesized positive and significant impact of perceived service quality, and customer satisfaction, as supported by the research conducted by Namkung & Jang, (2007). Customer Satisfaction leads to repurchase intentions of the customers, similar to the results of past research of a tourism study by Baker and Crompton (2000), which resulted as, service quality and customer satisfaction has an important role in explaining customer repurchase intentions toward restaurants.

The finding of the current study has resulted that customer satisfaction mediates the relationship between perceived service quality and repurchase intentions in restaurant industry of Pakistan. The mediation result support previous researchers' arguments about the mediating role of customer satisfaction affecting the repurchase intentions (Howard & Sheth, 1969).

Results proves that customer satisfaction has an impact on perceived service quality and customer loyalty; this is suggested the service managers should identify frequent visitors, their choices & characteristics, and devise multiple marketing strategies in order to capture the loyal customers. Pong, Johny & Tang , (2001) has suggested in their study that by providing information to their customers about new services offered and value added services which other restaurants are not offering; service manager can grab the attention of their customers and create loyalty. Moreover, different promotions, coupons and incentives can help the service manager in making the customers feel that the services which are being offered are the best than other restaurants. Such strategies will lead to a favorable attitude of the customer towards the restaurant and its services and will lead to repurchase intentions.

In comparison to other services, restaurant service providers need to pay more attention on the attributes e.g. whether their restaurant is in the evoke set of mind of their customers or not? Is it the first choice of the customers? This is essential to devise strategies which make their customers feel delighted and pleased after using the services.

Managerial Implications

The research has mainly focused on the effect of perceived service quality on customer loyalty and repurchases intention with the mediating role of customer satisfaction. The findings of this study are of great importance for all the service providers in specific the food industry and other services industries and companies in general. This can serve as a guide to all the service providers and can inform them about what measures they should take to improve their service quality and in return gain the desired customer loyalty. The findings of this study also emphasize that only good perceive service quality is not going to ensure the desired customer loyalty in fact we also need to consider the mediating effect of customer satisfaction to gain long term customer loyalty. The service organizations and their managers should ensure that they give their customers the desired personal attention and the customers should be highly satisfied at all the times. In order to ensure the desired customer satisfaction the companies need to ensure that their staff is well trained and are experienced enough to deal with the customers. The human factor or the human element is very important in the case of services that are outcome dominant. The services like restaurant dining is such in which the service quality of the restaurant is gauged by the customer with the help of service provided and the type of environment that the place provides, therefore a comfortable and neat and clean environment is essential viz-a-viz tasty food for the customer satisfaction and loyalty.

The study has also indicated that once the customer is happy with the service quality and is satisfied he is going to have a favorable attitude towards the service provider and will eventually like to repurchase from the service provider. Thus we can safely say that the good service quality not only generates the long term loyalty in the customers it also leads to the all important aspect of repurchase intention within the customer.

The assessment also provides the service providers with the detail of the loyal customers that they have and how they can improve their segmentation strategy basing on the number of loyal customers that they have in their particular area of interest. As far as the restaurant owners are concerned they need to ensure that their restaurant is the first choice amongst the customers that can be achieved only by continuously improving the service quality and in return the customer satisfaction.

Limitations and Future Research

In our research the biggest limitation or the problem that we faced was that we did not have direct access to the research journals or the relevant articles available with most of the educational institutions across the world. The respondents from whom we collected the data were not very cooperative due to which our data set was reduced to 230 although we had planned to have a data set of approximately 300.

This study focuses only on the marketing variables that include Perceived Service Quality, Customer Satisfaction, Customer Loyalty and Repurchase Intentions, there are few other marketing factors or variables that are omitted which can be used to further highlight the interconnection within these variables. The effect of staff behavior on customer loyalty could be one such example. The study on this side can further highlight the importance of service quality and customer satisfaction.

6. REFERENCES

References

Athanassopoulos, A. D., (2000). Customer satisfaction cues to support market segmentation & explain switching behavior. *Journal of Business Research, 47*, 191-207.

Anderson, E. W., Fornell, C & Lehmann, D. R., (1994). Customer satisfaction market share and profitability: Findings from Sweden. *Journal of Marketing, 58*, 53-66.

Armstrong, G. & Kotler, P., (1996). *Principles of marketing* (seventh edn.), Prentice Hall, India.

Andreassen, T. W., & Lindestad, B., (1998). Customer loyalty and complex services. *International Journal of Service Industry Management, 9*, 7-23.

Baker, D. A. & Crompton, J. L., (2000). Quality, satisfaction and behavioral intentions. *Annals of Tourism Research, 27*, 785-804.

Bagozzi, R. P., & Philips, L. W., (1982). Representing and testing organizational theories. A Holistic Construal. *Administrative science quarterly, 27*, 459-489.

Bearden, W. O., & Jesse, E. T., (1983). Selected determinants of customer satisfaction and complaint reports. *Journal of Marketing, 20*, 21-8.

Bloemer, J. M. M., & Kasper, H. D. P., (1995). The complex relationship between consumer satisfaction and brand loyalty. *Journal of Economic Psychology, 16*, 311-329.

Blanchard, R. F., & Galloway, R. L., (1994). Quality in retail banking. *International Journal of Service Industry Management, 5*, 5-23.

Bolton, R. N., (1998). A dynamic model of the duration of the customer's relationship with a continuous service provider: The Role of Satisfaction. *Marketing science, 17*, 45-65.

Boeselie, P., Hesselink, M., & Wiele, T. V., (2002). Empirical evidence for the relationship between customer satisfaction and business performance. *Managing service quality, 12*, 184-193.

Boulding, W. K. A., Staelin, R. & Zeithaml, V. A. (1993). A dynamic process model of service quality: from expectations to behavioural intentions. *Journal of Marketing Research, 30,* 7-27.

Caruana, A., (2002). Service loyalty: The effects of service quality and the mediating role of customer satisfaction. *European Journal of Marketing, 36,* 811-828.

Cronin, J. J., & Taylor, S. A., (1992a). Measuring service quality: a re-examination and extension. *Journal of Marketing, 56,* 55-68.

Cronin, J. J., & Taylor, S. A., (1992b). Measuring Service Quality: A Reexamination and Extension. *Journal of Marketing, 3,* 55-68.

Cronin, J. J., & Taylor, S. A., (1992c) Measuring service quality: A Reexamination and extension. *Journal of Marketing, 56,* 55–68.

Clark, M. A., & Wood, R. C., (1998). Consumer loyalty in the restaurant industry – a preliminary exploration of the issues. *International Journal of Contemporary Hospitality Management, 10,* 139-144.

Cunningham, R. M., (1956). Brand loyalty – what, where, how much? *Harvard Business Review, 39,* 116-138.

Czepiel, J. A. & Gilmore, R., (1987). Exploring the concept of loyalty in services. *Services marketing challenge: Integrating for competitive advantage,* 91-94.

Czepiel, J. A., & Gilmore, R., (1987). Exploring the concept of loyalty in services. In J. A. Czepiel, C. A. Congram, & J. Shanahan (Eds.), The services challenge: Integrating for competitive advantage 91–94. Chicago. IL: *American Marketing Association.*

Cronin, J. J., Brady, M. K., & Hult, T. M., (2000). Assessing the effects of quality, value and customer satisfaction on consumer behavioral intentions in science environments. *Journal of Retailing, 76,* 193-218.

Dawes, J., & Swailes, S., (1999). Retention sans frontieres: Issues for financial service retailers. *International Journal of Bank Marketing, 17,* 36-43.

Day, R. L., (1984). Modeling choices among alternative responses to dissatisfaction. *Advances in consumer research, 11.* Thomas C.K., ed. Ann Arbor, MI: Assosiation for Consumer Research, 496-9

Day, R. L., & Landon, Jr. E. L., (1977). Toward a theory of consumer complaining behavior. *Consumer and industrial buying behavior,* Arch G. Woodside, JagdishSheth, and Peter Bennett, eds. Elsevier North-Holland, 425-37.

De Ruyter, K., Wetzels, M., & Van Birgelen, M., (1999). How do customers react to critical service encounters?: A cross-sectional perspective. *Total Quality Management, 10,* 1131-1145.

DeSouza, G., (1992). Designing a customer retention plan. *The Journal of Business Strategy,* 24-28.

Dick, A. S., & Basu, K., (1994a). Customer loyalty: toward an integrated conceptual framework. *Journal of the Academy of Marketing Science, 22,* 99-113.

Dick, A. S. & Basu, K., (1994b). Customer loyalty: toward an integrated conceptual framework. *Journal of the Academy of Marketing Science, 22,* 99-113.

Disney, J., (1999). Customer satisfaction and loyalty: The critical elements of service quality. *Total quality management, 10,* S491-S497.

Dotchin, J. A., & Oakland, J. S., (1994). Total Quality Management in Services Part 2: Service Quality. *International Journal of Quality & Reliability Management, 11,* 27-42.

Ehigie, B. O., (2006). Correlates of customer loyalty to their bank: a case study in Nigeria. *International Journal of Bank Marketing, 24,* 494-508.

Fornell, C., (1992). A national customer satisfaction barometer: The Swedish experience. *Journal of Marketing, 56,* 1-18.

Fornell, C., (1976). Consumer Input for Marketing Decisions: A Study of Corporate Departments for Consumer Affairs, 57-73.

Fornier, S., (1994). A Consumer-Based Relationship Framework for Strategic Brand Management, *published PhD dissertation, University of Florida.*

Fogli, L., (2006). *Customer Service Delivery.* San Francisco: Jossey-Bass.

Gremler, D. D., & Brown, S. W., (1996a). Service loyalty: Its nature, importance, and implications. In Edvardsson, B., Brown, S. W., Johnston, R. and Scheuing, E. E., eds., *Proceedings American Marketing Association,* 171- 180.

Gremler, D. D., & Brown, S. W., (1996b). Service loyalty; its nature, importance and implications. In Edvardsson, B., Brown, S.W., Johnston, R. and Scheuing, E. (Eds), QUIS V: Advancing Service Quality: A Global Perspective, *ISQA, New York,* 171-81.

Gremler, D. D., & Brown, S.W., (1996c). Service loyalty; its nature, importance and implications. In Edvardsson, B., Brown, S.W., Johnston, R. and Scheuing, E. (Eds), QUIS V: Advancing Service Quality: A Global Perspective, *ISQA, New York,* 171-81.

Goodman, J. A., & Malech, A. R., (1986). The role of service in effective marketing. In *Handbook of Modern Marketing,* McGraw-Hill, 88-3-88-13.

Guiltinan, J. P., (1989). A classification of switching costs with implications for relationship marketing. In Childers, T.L. and Bagozzi, R.P. (Eds), *AMA Winter Educators' Conference: Marketing Theory and Practice, AMA, Chicago,* 216-20.

Gotlieb, J. B., Grewal, D., & Brown, S. W., (1994). Consumer Satisfaction and Perceived Quality: Complementary or Divergent Constructs? *Journal of Applied Psychology,* 875-885.

Guolla, Michael, & Large, D, (1997). A quality-satisfaction-loyalty framework for government services. *Optimum, the Journal of Public Sector Management, 27,* 49-57.

Grönroos, C., (2001). The perceived service quality concept - a mistake? *Managing Service Quality, 11,* 150-152.

Gronroos, C., (2000). Service Management and Marketing : A Customer Relationship Management Approach. 2nd ed. West Sussex: John Wiley & Sons, Ltd.

Hart, C. W., & Johnson, M. D., (1999). Growing the trust relationship. *Marketing Management, 14,* 8-19.

Hallowell, R., (1996a). The relationships of customer satisfaction, customer loyalty, and profitability: An empirical study. *International Journal of Service Industry Management, 7,* 27-42.

Hallowell, R., (1996b). The relationships of customer satisfaction, customer loyalty, and profitability: An empirical study. *International Journal of Service Industry Management, 7,* 27-42.

Hackl, P., Scharitzer, D., & Zuba, R., (2000). Customer satisfaction in the Austrian food retail market. *Total quality management, 1,* 999-1006.

Howard, J. A., (1974). The Structure of Buyer Behavior. In *Customer Behaviour: Theory and Application*, John V. Farley, John A. Howard, and L. Winston Ring, eds. Boston: Allyn & Bacon, 9-32.

Howard, J. A., & Sheth, J. N., (1969). the *Theory of Buyer Behaviour*, New York: John Wiley & Sons, Inc.

Honomichl, J., (1993). Spending on Customer Satisfaction Continues to Rise. *Marketing News*, *12*, 17-18.

Iacobuci, D., Grayson, K. A., & Ostrom A. L., (1994). The calculus of service quality and customer satisfaction: "Theoretical and Empirical Differentiation and Integration" In Swartz, A., Bowen D.E., & Brown S.W(eds.), Advances in Services Marketing and Management: *Research and Practice. JAI, Greenwich*.

Jacoby, J., & Kyner, D. B., (1973). Brand loyalty vs. Repeat purchasing behavior. *Journal of Marketing Research*, 1-9.

Jacoby, J., & Chestnut, R. W., (1978). *Brand Loyalty: Measurement and Management*. John Wiley and Sons, Inc., New York, 157.

Jones, T. O., & Sasser Jr., W. E., (1995). Why satisfied customer defect. *Harvard Business Review*, *73*, 88-99.

Keaveney, S. M., (1995). Customer switching behavior in service industries: an exploratory study. *Journal of Marketing*, *59*, 71-82.

Klemperer, P., (1987). Markets with consumer switching costs. *The Quarterly Journal of Economics*, *102*, 375-94.

La Barbera, P. A., & Mazursky, D., (1983). A longitudinal assessment of consumer satisfaction/dissatisfaction: The Dynamic Aspect of the Cognitive Process. *Journal of Marketing Research, 20*, 393-404.

Levesque, T. J., & McDougall, G. H. G., (1996). Determinants of customer satisfaction in retail banking. *International Journal of Bank Marketing, 14*, 12-20.

Lymperopoulos, C., Chaniotakis, I. E., & Soureli, M., (2006). The importance of service quality in bank selection for mortgage loans. *Managing Service Quality, 16*, 365-379.

Loveman, G. W., (1998). Employee satisfaction, customer loyalty, and financial performance. *Journal of Service Research, 1*, 18-31. Luk, T. K. S., (1999). The contribution of the outcome dimension to room service quality. Forthcoming paper in *International Journal of Hospitality Management* .

Lovelock, C. & Wright L., (1999). *Principles of Service Marketing and Management*. Prentice Hall, Englewood Cliffs.

Lee, J., Lee, J., & Feick, L., (2001). The impact of switching costs on the customer satisfaction-loyalty link: Mobile phone service in France. *Journal of Service Marketing, 15*, 35-48.

Pong, L. T., Johny, & Dr. Tang Pui Yee, E., (2001). An integrated model of service loyalty. *Academy of business & administrative sciences, International conferences, Belgium,* 23-25/

Macintosh, G. & Lockshin, L. S., (1998). Retail relationships and store loyalty; a multilevel perspective. *International Journal of Research in Marketing, 14*, 487-98.

Morgan, D. L., (1997). *Focus Groups as Qualitative Research*. Sage Publication: Qualitative Research Series, *16,* Second edition *80*, 52. Newman, J. W., (1973), & Werbel, R. A.,

Multivariate analysis of brand loyalty for major household appliances. *Journal of Marketing Research, 10*, 404-409.

Mittal, V., Ross, W. T., & Baldasare P. M., (1998). The asymmetric impact of negative and positive attribute-level performance on overall satisfaction and repurchase intentions, *Journal of Marketing, 1*, 33-47.

Mudie, P., & Pirrie, A., (2006). *Services Marketing Management.* 3rd ed. Oxford : Elsevier Ltd.

Narayandas, N., (1996). The link between customer satisfaction and customer loyalty: an empirical investigation Working Paper, *97-017, Harvard Business School*, Boston, MA.

Neal,W. D., (1999). Satisfaction is nice, but value drives loyalty. *Marketing Research*, 21–23.

Oliver, R. L., (1980). A cognitive model of the antecedents and consequences of satisfaction decisions. *Journal of Marketing Research, 17*, 460-9.

Oliver, R. L., (1997). Satisfaction: A Behavioral Perspective on the Consumer. New York: McGraw-Hill.

Oliver, R. L., (1980). A cognitive model of the antecedents and consequences of satisfaction decisions. *Journal of Marketing Research, 17*, 460-469.

Oliver, R. L., (1993). Cognitive, affective and attribute bases of the satisfaction response. *Journal of Consumer Research, 20*, 418–430.

Oliver, R. L., (1999). Whence consumer loyalty? *Journal of Marketing, 63*, 33-44.

O' Malley, L., (1988). Can loyalty schemes really build loyalty? *Marketing Intelligence & Planning, 16,* 47-55.

Pearson, N., (1996). Building brands directly: creating business value from customer Relationships. *Macmillan Business, 20*, 68-82.

Parasuraman, A., Zeithaml, V. A., & Berry, L. L., (1994). Reassessment of expectations as a comparison standard in measuring service quality: Implications for further research, *Journal of Marketing*, *1*, 111-124.

Parasuraman, A., Zeithamal, V. A., & Berry, L. L., (1988). SERVQUAL: A multiple-item scale for marketing consumer perceptions of service. *Journal of Retailing*, *64*, 12-40.

Parasuraman, A., Berry L. L., & Zeithaml, V. A., (1988). SERVQUAL : A multiple-item scale for measuring consumer perceptions of service quality. *Journal of Retailing, 64*, 12.

Parasuraman, A., Zeithaml, V. A., & Berry, L. L., (1988). SERVQUAL: A multiple-item scale for measuring consumer perceptions of service quality. *Journal of Retailing*, *64*, 12-40

Parasuraman, A., Zeithaml, V. A., & Berry, L. L., (1985). A conceptual model of service quality and its implications for future research. *Journal of Marketing*, *49*, 41-50.

Parasuraman, A., Zeithaml, V. A., & Berry, L. L., (1985). A conceptual model of service quality and its implications for future research. *Journal of Marketing*, *49*, 41-50.

Reichheld, F. F., (1996). Learning from customer defections *Harvard Business Review*, *74*, 56–67.

Richins, M. L., (1983). Negative word of mouth by dissatisfied customers: A pilot study. *Journal of Marketing*, *47*, 68-78.

Reichheld, F., (1996). The loyalty effect: The hidden force behind growth, profits, and lasting value. Boston: *Harvard Business School Press.Wall Street Journal (1998)*, "Business Plan," *19*), R18.

Reichheld, F. F., & Sasser Jr, W. E., (1990). Zero defections comes to services. *Harvard Business Review*, 105-11.

Reichheld, F. F., (1993). Loyalty-based management. *Harvard Business Review*, *71*, 64-73.

Shemwell, D. J., Yavas, U., & Bilgin, Z., (1998). Customer-service provider relationships: An empirical test of a model of service quality, satisfaction and relationship-oriented outcomes. *International Journal of Service Industry Management, 9*, 155-168.

Singh, J., (1991). Understanding the structure of consumers' satisfaction evaluations of service delivery. *Journal of the Academy of Marketing Science, 20*, 223-44.

Snyder, D. R., (1986). Service loyalty and its measurement: a preliminary investigation. In Venkatesan, M., Schmalensee, D. M., & Marshall, C. (Eds), Creativity in Service Marketing: What's New, What Works, What's Developing, *AMA, Chicago*, 44-8.

Spreng, R. A., & Mackoy R. D., (1996). An empirical examination of a model of perceived service quality and satisfaction. *Journal of Retailing*, 201-214.

Sureshchanndra, G. S., Rajendran, C. & Anantharaman, R. N., (2002). The relationship between service quality and customer loyalty - a factor specific approach. *Journal of Service Marketing, 16,* 363-379.

Taylor, S. A., & Baker T. L., (1994). An assessment of the relationship between service quality and customer satisfaction in the formation of consumer's purchase intentions. *Journal of Retailing, 2*, 163-178.

Westbrook, R. A., (1978). Product/Consumption based affective responses and post purchase process. *Journal of Marketing Research, 24*, 258-70.

Yi, Y., (1990). A critical review of customer satisfaction, in Zeithmal, V.(Ed.). *Review of Marketing, American Marketing Association*, Chicago, 68-123.

Namkung, Y., & Jang, S. C., (2007). Does food quality really matter in restaurants? Its impact on customer satisfaction and behavioral intentions. *Journal of Hospitality & Tourism Research, 31,* 387-409.

Zeithaml, V. A., Parasuraman, A., & Berry, L. L., (1990). Delivering quality service. *The Free Press, New York*, NY.

Zeithaml, V. A., (1981). How consumer evaluation processes differ between goods and services. In Donnelly, J. H., & George, W. R., (Eds). *Marketing of Services, AMA, Chicago,* 186-90.

Zeithaml, V. A., Berry, L. L., & Parasuraman, A., (1996). The behavioral consequences of Service quality. *Journal of Marketing, 60,* 31-46.

Zeithaml, V. A., & Bitner, M. J., (1996). *Services Marketing*, McGraw-Hill, New York, NY.

APPENDIX –A

Respected Sir/Madam,

We are research students at Faculty of Management Sciences (**MBA**) at University of Central Punjab, Lahore. We are working on our Research Methodology project. We need your valued time and coordination with us to create knowledge. We ensure you that any information obtained in connection with this study, will remain highly confidential. In any written report or publication, no one will be identified and only aggregate data will be presented.

Income : ☐ 15-30 Thousand ☐ 30-45 Thousand ☐ 45-60 Thousand ☐ Above 60 thousand		
Gender :	**Qualification :**	
Age :	**Occupation :**	

The following statements concern your perception about variety of Companies. Select a brand of these below and please indicate the extent of your agreement and disagreement by ticking (√) the appropriate number.

Restaurants

Village ☐	Dhabba ☐	Fazal-e-Haq ☐	PizzaHut ☐
Hsin Kong ☐	Mei Kong ☐	Bundu Khan ☐	Nandos ☐

Scale

Strongly Disagree	Disagree	Somewhat Disagree	Neutral	Somewhat Agree	Agree	Strongly Agree
1	2	3	4	5	6	7

1. Your Restaurant has up-to date Equipment.

1. Strongly Disagree 2. Disagree 3. Somewhat disagree 4.Neutral 5.Somewhat Agree 6. Agree 7.Strongly Agree

2. Restaurant's physical facilities are visually appealing.

1. Strongly Disagree 2. Disagree 3. Somewhat disagree 4.Neutral 5.Somewhat Agree 6. Agree 7.Strongly Agree

3. Restaurant workers and other Staff members are well dressed and appear neat.

1. Strongly Disagree 2. Disagree 3. Somewhat disagree 4.Neutral 5.Somewhat Agree 6. Agree 7.Strongly Agree

4. Material associated with the service (like computers, LCD TV, dining place and infrastructure) is   visually appealing.

1. Strongly Disagree 2. Disagree 3. Somewhat disagree 4.Neutral 5.Somewhat Agree 6. Agree 7.Strongly Agree

5. When your restaurant promises to do something by a certain time, so it does so.

1. Strongly Disagree 2. Disagree 3. Somewhat disagree 4.Neutral 5.Somewhat Agree 6. Agree 7.Strongly Agree

6. When you have some problems (regarding service), restaurant shows a sincere interest in solving it.

1. Strongly Disagree 2. Disagree 3. Somewhat disagree 4.Neutral 5.Somewhat Agree 6. Agree 7.Strongly Agree

7. Restaurant performs the service right (accurate) the first time.

1. Strongly Disagree 2. Disagree 3. Somewhat disagree 4.Neutral 5.Somewhat Agree 6. Agree 7.Strongly Agree

8. Restaurant provides services at a time, it promises to do so.

1. Strongly Disagree 2. Disagree 3. Somewhat disagree 4.Neutral 5.Somewhat Agree 6. Agree 7.Strongly Agree

9. Restaurant keeps its record accurately.

1. Strongly Disagree 2. Disagree 3. Somewhat disagree 4.Neutral 5.Somewhat Agree 6. Agree 7.Strongly Agree

10. Workers and other staff members of restaurant tell you exactly when the services will be performed.

1. Strongly Disagree 2. Disagree 3. Somewhat disagree 4.Neutral 5.Somewhat Agree 6. Agree 7.Strongly Agree

11. Workers and others staff members of this restaurant give you on time service.

1. Strongly Disagree 2. Disagree 3. Somewhat disagree 4.Neutral 5.Somewhat Agree 6. Agree 7.Strongly Agree

12. Workers and other staff members of this restaurant always willing to help you.

1. Strongly Disagree 2. Disagree 3. Somewhat disagree 4.Neutral 5.Somewhat Agree 6. Agree 7.Strongly Agree

13. Workers and other staff members of restaurant are never too busy to respond to your request.

1. Strongly Disagree 2. Disagree 3. Somewhat disagree 4.Neutral 5.Somewhat Agree 6. Agree 7.Strongly Agree

14. The behavior of workers and other staff members instills (encourage) confidence in consumers.

1. Strongly Disagree 2. Disagree 3. Somewhat disagree 4.Neutral 5.Somewhat Agree 6. Agree 7.Strongly Agree

15. You feel safe to take the services from this restaurant.

1. Strongly Disagree 2. Disagree 3. Somewhat disagree 4.Neutral 5.Somewhat Agree 6. Agree 7.Strongly Agree

16. Workers and other staff members of this restaurant are consistently courteous with you.

1. Strongly Disagree 2. Disagree 3. Somewhat disagree 4.Neutral 5.Somewhat Agree 6. Agree 7.Strongly Agree

17. Your restaurant gives you individual attention.

1. Strongly Disagree 2. Disagree 3. Somewhat disagree 4.Neutral 5.Somewhat Agree 6. Agree 7.Strongly Agree

18. Restaurant workers and staff members have the knowledge to answer your question.

1. Strongly Disagree 2. Disagree 3. Somewhat disagree 4.Neutral 5.Somewhat Agree 6. Agree 7.Strongly Agree

19. Restaurant operating hours is convenient to all the consumers.

1. Strongly Disagree 2. Disagree 3. Somewhat disagree 4.Neutral 5.Somewhat Agree 6. Agree 7.Strongly Agree

20. Restaurant workers and other staff members give you personal attention.

1. Strongly Disagree 2. Disagree 3. Somewhat disagree 4.Neutral 5.Somewhat Agree 6. Agree 7.Strongly Agree

21. Restaurant has the best interest at heart.

1. Strongly Disagree 2. Disagree 3. Somewhat disagree 4.Neutral 5.Somewhat Agree 6. Agree 7.Strongly Agree

22. Workers and other staff members of restaurant understand your specific needs.

1. Strongly Disagree 2. Disagree 3. Somewhat disagree 4.Neutral 5.Somewhat Agree 6. Agree 7.Strongly Agree

23. Is the restaurant staff courteous?

1. Strongly Disagree 2. Disagree 3. Somewhat disagree 4.Neutral 5.Somewhat Agree 6. Agree 7.Strongly Agree

24. The service provided by the restaurant is on time.

1. Strongly Disagree 2. Disagree 3. Somewhat disagree 4.Neutral 5.Somewhat Agree 6. Agree 7.Strongly Agree

25. Are the employees competent?

1. Strongly Disagree 2. Disagree 3. Somewhat disagree 4.Neutral 5.Somewhat Agree 6. Agree 7.Strongly Agree

26. Is the staff helpful.

1. Strongly Disagree 2. Disagree 3. Somewhat disagree 4.Neutral 5.Somewhat Agree 6. Agree 7.Strongly Agree

27. Are the operating hours convenient to the customers.

1. Strongly Disagree 2. Disagree 3. Somewhat disagree 4.Neutral 5.Somewhat Agree 6. Agree 7.Strongly Agree

28. Is the restaurant neat and clean?

1. Strongly Disagree 2. Disagree 3. Somewhat disagree 4.Neutral 5.Somewhat Agree 6. Agree 7.Strongly Agree

29. Is the treatment received good and up to standard?

1. Strongly Disagree 2. Disagree 3. Somewhat disagree 4.Neutral 5.Somewhat Agree 6. Agree 7.Strongly Agree

30. Is the service and staff easy to access?

1. Strongly Disagree 2. Disagree 3. Somewhat disagree 4.Neutral 5.Somewhat Agree 6. Agree 7.Strongly Agree

31. Do the employees listen to you?

1. Strongly Disagree 2. Disagree 3. Somewhat disagree 4.Neutral 5.Somewhat Agree 6. Agree 7.Strongly Agree

32. Is the security environment good within the organization?

1. Strongly Disagree 2. Disagree 3. Somewhat disagree 4.Neutral 5.Somewhat Agree 6. Agree 7.Strongly Agree

33. Are the security measures used outside organization up to mark?

1. Strongly Disagree 2. Disagree 3. Somewhat disagree 4.Neutral 5.Somewhat Agree 6. Agree 7.Strongly Agree

34. Is the help offered by employees prompt?

1. Strongly Disagree 2. Disagree 3. Somewhat disagree 4.Neutral 5.Somewhat Agree 6. Agree 7.Strongly Agree

35. Is the service cost reasonable?

1. Strongly Disagree 2. Disagree 3. Somewhat disagree 4.Neutral 5.Somewhat Agree 6. Agree 7.Strongly Agree

36. Is the treatment offered by staff fair?

1. Strongly Disagree 2. Disagree 3. Somewhat disagree 4.Neutral 5.Somewhat Agree 6. Agree 7.Strongly Agree

37. Does the organization deliver what it promises?

1. Strongly Disagree 2. Disagree 3. Somewhat disagree 4.Neutral 5.Somewhat Agree 6. Agree 7.Strongly Agree

38. Are the staff personnel helpful?

1. Strongly Disagree 2. Disagree 3. Somewhat disagree 4.Neutral 5.Somewhat Agree 6. Agree 7.Strongly Agree

39. Does the management backs up what it promises.

1. Strongly Disagree 2. Disagree 3. Somewhat disagree 4.Neutral 5.Somewhat Agree 6. Agree 7.Strongly Agree

40. I rarely (some time) consider switching to another restaurant.

1. Strongly Disagree 2. Disagree 3. Somewhat disagree 4.Neutral 5.Somewhat Agree 6. Agree 7.Strongly Agree

41. As long as the present service continues, I doubt that I would switch restaurant.

1. Strongly Disagree 2. Disagree 3. Somewhat disagree 4.Neutral 5.Somewhat Agree 6. Agree 7.Strongly Agree

42. I try to use this restaurant whenever I need to eat out.

1. Strongly Disagree 2. Disagree 3. Somewhat disagree 4.Neutral 5.Somewhat Agree 6. Agree 7.Strongly Agree

43. When I need to eat out, this restaurant is my first choice.

1. Strongly Disagree 2. Disagree 3. Somewhat disagree 4.Neutral 5.Somewhat Agree 6. Agree 7.Strongly Agree

44. I like using this restaurant.

1. Strongly Disagree 2. Disagree 3. Somewhat disagree 4.Neutral 5.Somewhat Agree 6. Agree 7.Strongly Agree

45. To me this restaurant is the best restaurant to do business with.

1. Strongly Disagree 2. Disagree 3. Somewhat disagree 4.Neutral 5.Somewhat Agree 6. Agree 7.Strongly Agree

46. I believe that this is my favorite restaurant.

1. Strongly Disagree 2. Disagree 3. Somewhat disagree 4.Neutral 5.Somewhat Agree 6. Agree 7.Strongly Agree

47. I intend to continue to be customer of this restaurant.

1. Strongly Disagree 2. Disagree 3. Somewhat disagree 4.Neutral 5.Somewhat Agree 6. Agree 7.Strongly Agree

48. Next time I shall need products/services of this restaurant I will buy it from here.

1. Strongly Disagree 2. Disagree 3. Somewhat disagree 4.Neutral 5.Somewhat Agree 6. Agree 7.Strongly Agree